POST-TRAUMATIC STRESS DISORDER WORKBOOK

Practical Help and Information for PTSD

SHERI MCLAUGHLIN, RPC, CPCA

POST-TRAUMATIC STRESS DISORDER WORKBOOK
Copyright © 2017 by Sheri McLaughlin, RPC, CPCA

The information outlined in this workbook is the result of decades of experience and research by the author. It is intended to provide practical and helpful information regarding the subject of post-traumatic stress disorder. Any use of the information in this book is at the reader's discretion. The author and publisher specifically disclaim any and all liability arising directly or indirectly from the use or application of any information contained in this book.

Every effort has been made to ensure that the information contained herein is accurate. The ideas, procedures, and suggestions contained in this book are not intended as a substitute for consulting with a medical doctor or psychological health care professional.

ISBN: 978-1-4866-1489-9

Word Alive Press
131 Cordite Road, Winnipeg, MB R3W 1S1
www.wordalivepress.ca

Cataloguing in Publication may be obtained through Library and Archives Canada

CONTENTS

As a person who has personally suffered from PTSD, anxiety, depression, and panic attacks, I find it unhelpful to be labelled as someone with a mental illness. For me, I felt kind of odd and wondered why I just couldn't get on with my life. I would hear about murders on the news and often the perpetrator would be described as someone who had a mental illness. I didn't want to be labelled in the same category and it greatly disturbed me.

I am choosing to describe PTSD as a struggle with our emotions due to circumstances we were unable to control. We would not have chosen to have traumas inflicted upon us.

In my opinion, the healing process related to PTSD, depression, anxiety, and other emotional issues isn't much different from the healing process in regards to physical injuries. The brain is a physical part of our makeup, just as any other part of our body. The brain encompasses our minds and our emotions. If we have an injury here, it only makes sense that we will experience difficulty with our emotions and thought processes.

If you broke your arm or leg, likely you would have a cast put on, and it would take a great deal of time to heal. There is no cast for our emotions, and very often we (or others) put ourselves under a lot of pressure and unrealistic expectations to get well quickly.

This workbook has been produced to enable you in the healing process. It is also designed to give you measurable progress in your journey towards wholeness. I think you will be encouraged to know that there are people out there who understand what you've been through.

Please be encouraged that there is a way out to a full, meaningful, productive life full of peace and joy.

CHAPTER ONE

What Is Post-Traumatic Stress Disorder (PTSD)?

It is important to understand the specific changes in the Diagnostic and Statistical Manual of Mental Disorders, 5th Edition (DSM-5)[1] in defining PTSD. It is no longer classified as an anxiety disorder. Language stipulating an individual's response to an event (intense fear, helplessness, or horror) has been deleted because that criterion has proved to have no utility in predicting the onset of PTSD. The condition is now classified as a trauma and stress-related disorder.

Instead of three major symptom clusters for PTSD, the DSM-5 now lists four clusters:

Re-experiencing (previously called "intrusive recollection,")—involves the persistent re-experiencing of the experience through thoughts or perceptions, images, dreams, illusions or hallucinations, dissociative flashback episodes or intense psychological distress or reactivity to cues that symbolize some aspect of the event.

Avoidance (previously called "avoidant/numbing")—involves avoidance of stimuli that are associated with the trauma and numbing of general responsiveness. This is determined by avoidance of thoughts, feelings, or conversations associated with the event and /or avoidance of people, places, or activities that may trigger recollections of the event.

Negative cognitions and mood (new in the DSM-5)—involves negative alterations in thought and mood as characterized by symptoms like: inability to remember an important aspect of the event(s), persistent negative emotional state, persistent inability to experience positive emotions and others.

Arousal (previously called "hyper-arousal")—involves alteration in arousal and reactivity. Examples of this include: irritable behavior and angry outbursts, reckless or self-destructive

---

1   American Psychiatric Association, *Diagnostic and Statistical Manual of Mental Disorders, 5th Edition (DSM-5)* (Arlington, VA: American Psychiatric Association Publishing, 2013).

behavior, hypervigilance, exaggerated startle response, concentration problems, and/or sleep disturbance.[2]

PTSD STARTS WITH A STRESSOR (THE EVENT)

Criterion A (one required): The person was exposed to: death, threatened death, actual or threatened serious injury, or actual or threatened sexual violence, in the following way(s):

- Direct exposure
- Witnessing the trauma
- Learning that a relative or close friend was exposed to a trauma
- Indirect exposure to aversive details of the trauma, usually in the course of professional duties (e.g., first responders, medics)

Criterion B (one required): The traumatic event is persistently re-experienced, in the following way(s):

- Intrusive thoughts
- Nightmares
- Flashbacks
- Emotional distress after exposure to traumatic reminders
- Physical reactivity after exposure to traumatic reminders

Criterion C (one required): Avoidance of trauma-related stimuli after the trauma, in the following way(s):

- Trauma-related thoughts or feelings
- Trauma-related reminders

Criterion D (two required): Negative thoughts or feelings that began or worsened after the trauma, in the following way(s):

- Inability to recall key features of the trauma
- Overly negative thoughts and assumptions about oneself or the world
- Exaggerated blame of self or others for causing the trauma
- Negative affect

---

2   Harry Croft, M.D., *Healthy Place*, "How Did PTSD Change from the DSM-IV to the DSM-5?" December 18, 2013 2013 (https://www.healthyplace.com/blogs/understandingcombatptsd/2013/12/ptsd-change-dsm-iv-dsm-5).

- Decreased interest in activities
- Feeling isolated
- Difficulty experiencing positive affect

Criterion E (two required): Trauma-related arousal and reactivity that began or worsened after the trauma, in the following way(s):

- Irritability or aggression
- Risky or destructive behavior
- Hypervigilance
- Heightened startle reaction
- Difficulty concentrating
- Difficulty sleeping[3]

Note:

The DSM-5 also includes two new subtypes of PTSD: PTSD Preschool and PTSD Dissociative. Although it is beyond the scope of this workbook to discuss in detail the subtypes, I mention them because it is critical to understand them.

What is a trauma?

- An event outside normal human experience; a situation beyond your control.
- An event where ordinary coping skills are completely overwhelmed and useless.

What are some general facts about trauma?

- It shakes a person to the core.
- It creates gut reactions produced by automatic responses that are encoded into the brain's implicit memory system.
- It has a huge impact on how a person does life.
- It may not even be remembered, but it can still influence people's behavior.
- It causes profound and lasting changes in a person's emotion, cognition, and memory long after the traumatic experience has occurred.
- It strips a person of their sense of power and control, causing them to experience a horrific loss of safety.
- It can cause impairments to the linkages in the brain.

---

3   *U.S. Department of Veterans Affairs*, "PTSD: National Cener for PTSD." February 21, 2017 (https://www.ptsd.va.gov/professional/PTSD-overview/dsm5_criteria_ptsd.asp).

- It often causes people to feel as if they are losing their mind.

How are traumatic memories stored in the brain?

- The memories are dissociated.
- The memories are not assembled into a story or narrative.
- The memories are not a piece of one's autobiography.
- The memories can be suppressed.

Examples of traumatic events:

- rape
- sexual molestation
- military combat
- violent personal assaults
- automobile accidents
- airplane crashes

- terrorist attacks
- torture
- natural disasters
- observing the serious injury or unnatural death of another person

---

Notes:

- While the event causing the trauma is abnormal, PTSD is a normal human response to an abnormal situation.
- Post-traumatic stress can actually be a helpful mechanism for responding to threats to one's personal safety.
- What happened to you was *not* normal, but you *are* normal.

SYMPTOMS OF PTSD

This information in regards to PTSD symptoms is not intended for self-diagnosis. If you can relate to any of the following symptoms listed herein, please consult with your medical doctor and psychological health care provider.

The following is a list of general symptoms of PTSD. Please check all that apply to you:

- ☐ persistent re-experiencing of the event
- ☐ intense psychological reactivity to cues that symbolize some aspect of the event
- ☐ insomnia/sleep disturbances
- ☐ difficulty concentrating
- ☐ having a hard time completing tasks

- ☐ preoccupation with the event
- ☐ a lack of interest in one's usual activities
- ☐ abandonment of self-care
- ☐ withdrawal from others
- ☐ an inability to trust others
- ☐ substance abuse

☐ indecisiveness
☐ intrusive thoughts or perceptions
☐ irritability/anger
☐ flashbacks
☐ bad dreams/nightmares
☐ wanting to stay away from anything associated with the trauma

☐ depression
☐ anxiety
☐ making efforts to avoid thoughts, feelings, or conversations about the traumatic event
☐ worrying a lot that something else bad is going to happen

Questions About PTSD General Symptoms

1. How have these symptoms influenced your ability to live your life as you would like?

_____

_____

_____

2. Which symptoms would you like to start working on right away?

_____

_____

_____

3. What are some changes you could implement into your life to get the help you need?

_____

_____

_____

The following is a list of physiological reactions of PTSD. Please check all that apply to you:

☐ heartbeat irregularities
☐ headaches
☐ hyperventilating
☐ sweating (which originates in the mind through mental or emotional conflict)

☐ chest pain
☐ digestive issues
☐ high blood pressure
☐ holding tension in one's body
☐ hypervigilance

☐ extreme fatigue or exhaustion   ☐ being jumpy or easily startled

☐ indigestion, nausea, and vomiting

Questions About PTSD Physical Symptoms

1. Have you spoken to your medical doctor about your symptoms?

_____

_____

_____

2. What changes could you make to your lifestyle to improve your physical well-being?

_____

_____

_____

3. What are some activities you could do to promote rest and relaxation?

_____

_____

_____

Suggestions for Maintaining Overall Physical Health

1. Maintain good nutrition.
2. Take supplements and/or medicines as required.
3. Exercise regularly.
4. Get regular rest and relaxation.
5. Get a proper amount of quality sleep.
6. Engage in progressive relaxation (the tensing and relaxing of muscles).
7. Breathe deeply from the diaphragm for five to ten minutes per day.

HONESTY VS. PLAY ACTING

When I'm sick, I get tired of it. You may know this feeling—being sick and tired of being sick and tired. So often, I'll try to live as if I'm not sick. I'll pretend I'm healthy enough to go on about my normal business. But that just sets me up for a relapse and spending more time in recovery than I otherwise would have needed. We need to give ourselves a break. The truth is that we need to be comfortable with just getting by sometimes, because sometimes that's the best we can do.[4]

A survivor is a person who, when knocked down, somehow knows to stay down until the count of nine and then gets up differently. The nonsurvivor gets up right away and gets hit again.[5]

In my own personal struggle in overcoming PTSD, I found that not taking enough time to heal from my traumas had an adverse effect on my health and wellbeing. By repressing my emotions, and through my unconscious ways of not dealing with the stressors in my life, I allowed myself to progress to the exhaustion stage of the General Adaptation Syndrome.[6] My body shut down and it took me the good part of a year to achieve full physical healing.

---

4   Thomas A. Whiteman, Ph.D. and Randy Petersen, *Becoming Your Own Best Friend* (Nashville, TN: Thomas Nelson, 1994), 40.

5   H. Norman Wright, *Recovering from Losses in Life* (Grand Rapids, MI: Revell, 2006), 127–128.

6   For more information about the General Adaptation Syndrome, see: Hans Selye, *Current Nursing*, "General Adaptation Syndrome (GAS): Theory of Stress." September 8, 2011 (http://www.currentnursing.com/nursing_theory/Selye's_stress_theory.html).

CHAPTER TWO

NEGATIVE COGNITION AND MOOD

WHAT EXACTLY IS AN EMOTION?

According to the book *Discovering Psychology*, "An emotion is a complex psychological state that involves three distinct components: a subjective experience, a physiological response, and a behavioral or expressive response."[7]

COMMON EMOTIONS OF PTSD

Negative alterations in thought and mood are characterized by symptoms such as those in the following list. Please check all that apply to you:

- ☐ emotional distress after exposure to traumatic reminders
- ☐ physical reactivity after exposure to traumatic reminders
- ☐ an inability to remember an important aspect of the event(s)
- ☐ an inability to recall key features of the trauma
- ☐ a persistent negative emotional state

- ☐ overly negative thoughts and assumptions about oneself or the world
- ☐ exaggerated blame of self or others for causing the trauma
- ☐ negative affect
- ☐ a decreased interest in activities
- ☐ difficulty experiencing positive affect
- ☐ anxiety
- ☐ irritability

---

7 D.H. Hockenburg and S.E. Hockenbury, *Discovering Psychology* (New York, NY: Worth Publishers). As excerpted from: Kendra Cherry, *Very Well*, "What Are Emotions and the Types of Emotional Responses?" July 21, 2017 (https://www.verywell.com/what-are-emotions-2795178).

☐ a persistent inability to experience positive emotions

☐ persistent, distorted cognitions about the cause or consequences of the event(s)

☐ concentration problems

☐ risky behavior

☐ reckless behavior

☐ self-destructive behavior

☐ hypervigilance

☐ an exaggerated startle response

☐ aggression

☐ avoidance of external reminders of the trauma

☐ avoidance of internal memories, thoughts, and feelings that remind one of the trauma

☐ avoidance of trauma-related thoughts or feelings

☐ avoidance of trauma-related reminders

☐ anger/angry outbursts

☐ panic

☐ depression

☐ fear

☐ phobias

☐ grief

☐ inappropriate regret

☐ despair

☐ feeling permanently damaged

☐ believing you are ineffective

☐ an inability to trust anyone

☐ dissociative symptoms

☐ feeling detached from others

☐ feeling isolated

☐ assuming that life will be unfulfilling

☐ self-blame

☐ false guilt

☐ shame

☐ feeling numb

Questions About Common PTSD Emotions

1. Have the responses you checked above affected the way you would like to live your life?

_____

_____

_____

2. Is there anything in the above list you would like to change?

_____

_____

_____

3. Have you spoken to anyone about your emotional struggles?

_____

_____

_____

FACTS ABOUT TRIGGERS, FLASHBACKS, NIGHTMARES, AND DISSOCIATION

Triggers	Flashbacks	Nightmares	Dissociation
Anything that reminds you of the trauma. Sensory input can include sights, sounds, smells, certain people, or personality types.	A kind of memory that is so powerful that it feels as if the present has faded away and you are actually back in the time and place of the traumatic event.	Repeated nightmares are very common.	Dissociation is the splitting off and isolation of memory imprints. It is the most direct psychological defense against overwhelming traumatic experiences.
These sensory inputs remind you of trauma through associative learning (meaning that your body and brain link things together through association).	Often you feel as though the trauma is happening all over again.	Many survivors say that they avoid going to bed because it means reliving the trauma through nightmares.	Dissociation prevents the trauma from being integrated into one's autobiography.
Your brain records things and makes associations and linkages, which form into "mental models."	Flashbacks can be terrifying and disorienting. They can be very hard on a person.	You may put off going to bed, or sleep in places that feel safer (i.e. under the bed or in a closet).	Dissociation is a mental and emotional way of removing yourself from the hurtful and dangerous present.

A past experience can powerfully influence your thoughts, feelings, and behavior without you being aware of how the past is influencing the present.	During a flashback, it is hard to hear anything in the present.	You may stay awake until sleep forces itself on you through sheer exhaustion.	You can dissociate so that you don't feel the physical sensations of the trauma in your body.
When you're triggered, traumatic memories become encoded in an abnormal form of memory, which breaks spontaneously into consciousness, both as flashbacks and nightmares.	The memory of the trauma can seem more real than what is happening in the present.	Nightmares can take the form of nightly replays of literal memories.	You can dissociate from your emotions so that you don't have to feel anything.
Emotions and physical sensations imprinted during the trauma are experienced as disruptive physical reactions, not as memories.	The people in the memory may appear more real than the people in the present.		You can disconnect from reality to the point that you are no longer aware of what is happening at all.
You can be triggered by certain emotions you feel in response to various situations.	The emotions you are feeling might not "mirror" reality.		

By discovering and keeping a record of your triggers and corresponding behavior, you can learn how to change your reactions and behavior.

In the following chart, identify your own personal triggers, flashbacks, nightmares, and ways in which you dissociate:

My Personal Triggers	The Flashbacks I Experience	Descriptions of My Nightmares	The Ways I Dissociate

French psychologist, philosopher, and psychotherapist Pierre Marie Felix Janet has been ranked along with William James and William Windt as being among the founding fathers of the field of psychology. In 1936, Janet also was given an honorary doctorate from Harvard.[8] In *The Body Keeps the Score*, author Bessel van der Kolk wrote,

> Janet coined the term "dissociate" to describe the splitting off and isolation of memory imprints that he saw in his patients. He predicted that unless they became aware of the split-off elements and integrated them into a story that had happened in the past but was now over, they would experience a slow decline in their personal and professional functioning. This phenomenon has now been well documented in contemporary research. Janet discovered that, while it is normal to change and distort one's memory, people with PTSD are unable to put the actual event, the source of those memories behind them.[9]

THE IMPORTANCE OF RENUNCIATION AND REPENTANCE

> Renounce: to say especially in a formal or official way that you will no longer have or accept (something); to formally give up (something)... to say in a formal or definite way that you refuse to follow, obey, or support (someone or something) any longer.[10]

The Bible teaches that "the one who conceals his sins does not prosper, but whoever confesses and renounces them finds mercy." Renounce means to forsake or say no to something or someone. Renounce is the first step toward repentance, which means to turn away from something and towards something else. Repentance literally means a change of mind, but it is much more comprehensive in its application.[11]

> Repent: to turn from sin and dedicate oneself to the amendment of one's life... to feel regret or contrition... to change one's mind.[12]

Repentance truly is your friend, and brain research proves it...But, humans as we are, I won't try to force the word "repent" on you. You can call it something else if you want. What I will try to do is to help you see the power of "getting it", which means really, really, really, really changing your mind about

---

8 *Wikipedia*, "Pierre Janet." Date of access: May 31, 2017 (https://en.wikipedia.org/wiki/Pierre_Janet).

9 Bessel van der Kolk, MD, *The Body Keeps the Score: Brain, Mind, and Body in the Healing of Trauma* (New York, NY: Penguin, 2015), 182.

10 *Merriam-Webster*, "Renounce." Date of access: April 10, 2017 (https://www.merriam-webster.com/dictionary/renounce).

11 Neil T. Anderson, *Restored: Experience Life with Jesus* (Franklin, TN: e3 Resources, 2007), 27.

12 *Merriam-Webster*, "Repent." Date of access: May 31, 2017 (https://www.merriam-webster.com/dictionary/repent).

some key realities that are keeping you from what you want out of life—personally or professionally—and turning from them."[13]

PRAYER

Heavenly Father, I am having flashbacks and/or nightmares about the trauma(s) that has been inflicted upon me. I renounce _____. Please release me from the torment and break the hold this event(s) has on me. In the powerful name of Jesus I pray, amen.

---

13 Dr. Henry Cloud, *Never Go Back: 10 Things You'll Never Do Again* (Brentwood, TN: Howard Books, 2014), 6, 8.

CHAPTER THREE

Losses

The following is a list of some of the losses you could have experienced. Please check all that apply to you:

- ☐ Someone you loved
- ☐ A significant relationship
- ☐ Hope
- ☐ A purpose
- ☐ Competence
- ☐ Ambition
- ☐ Adequacy
- ☐ Effectiveness
- ☐ Courage
- ☐ Strength
- ☐ Self-esteem
- ☐ A physical function
- ☐ A sense of control
- ☐ Peace
- ☐ Plans
- ☐ Dreams
- ☐ A role
- ☐ An identity
- ☐ Feeling safe

Possible Reasons for Not Grieving Our Losses

- We, or others, downplay the significance of our loss (minimization).
- We want to hold onto our loss so that we don't have to say goodbye.
- We are fearful that others will judge us.
- We don't want to face our loss.
- We have lost so much that we are overwhelmed and don't know where to start.
- We want to get back on with our lives as quickly as possible.

Life is full of losses. We have the choice of doing something constructive or destructive with our loss. Losses change you, so accepting your loss and learning to live with it is a process.

God, give me grace to accept with serenity
the things that cannot be changed,
Courage to change the things
which should be changed,
and the Wisdom to distinguish
the one from the other.
Living one day at a time,
Enjoying one moment at a time,
Accepting hardship as a pathway to peace,
Taking, as Jesus did,
This sinful world as it is,
Not as I would have it,
Trusting that You will make all things right,
If I surrender to Your will,
So that I may be reasonably happy in this life,
And supremely happy with You forever in the next.
Amen.[14]

Questions About Losses You Have Suffered

1. Have any of the above losses changed how you view yourself?

_____

_____

_____

2. Is there any kind of loss you've experienced that doesn't make sense, or over which you can't seem to get closure?

_____

_____

_____

3. Do you think you've fully grieved your losses?

_____

---

14 *Wikipedia*, "Serenity Prayer." Date of access: June 1, 2017 (https://en.wikipedia.org/wiki/Serenity_Prayer).

_____

_____

4. Do you feel as though you've lost "yourself"?

_____

_____

_____

If your brain believes you are helpless to change a situation, it can shut down. You might stop speaking up for yourself, stuff down your real feelings, and eventually find that your sense of self has disappeared. You switch to survival mode, which can cause emotional upheaval.

Survival mode activates the fight-or-flight response[15] and throws your nervous system out of whack. You can become overwhelmed, disorganized, and hypervigilant. The other extreme is that you can freeze and not participate in life. You go into depression and get stuck, withdrawing from people and activities that once provided enjoyment and fulfillment.

RECOVERING FROM LOSSES

Even if you attempt to ignore the loss, the emotional experience of it is implanted in your heart and mind, and no eraser will remove it…

The purpose of grieving over your loss is to get beyond these reactions to face your loss and work on adapting to it. The overall purpose of grief is to bring you to the point of making necessary changes so you can live with the loss in a healthy way…

For recovery to occur, we need to look back and say good-bye.[16]

PRAYER

Heavenly Father, I am really feeling the loss of _____. I do not know how to grieve in order that I may get well. Please help me heal in the areas where I am lacking. Please give me a sense of wholeness and help me to make sense of everything. I ask for Your wisdom in my journey toward complete restoration. Please give me the peace to accept what I cannot change. In Jesus' name, amen.

---

15 For more information about the fight-or-flight response, see: *Essence of Stress Relief*, "Hans Selye's General Adaptation Syndrome." Date of access: June 1, 2017 (http://www.essenceofstressrelief.com/general-adaptation-syndrome.html).

16 Wright, *Recovering from Losses in Life*, 11, 41, 91.

A Loss of Self: Who Are You, Really?

Then God said, "Let us make mankind in our image, in our likeness, so that they may rule over the fish in the sea and the birds in the sky, over the livestock and all the wild animals, and over all the creatures that move along the ground." So God created mankind in his own image, in the image of God he created them; male and female he created them. (Genesis 1:26–27)

From one man he made all the nations, that they should inhabit the whole earth; and he marked out their appointed times in history and the boundaries of their lands. God did this so that they would seek him and perhaps reach out for him and find him, though he is not far from any one of us. "For in him we live and move and have our being." As some of your own poets have said, "We are his offspring."

—Acts 17:26–28

…just as He chose us in Him before the foundation of the world, that we would be holy and blameless before Him. In love He predestined us to adoption as sons through Jesus Christ to Himself, according to the kind intention of His will… also we have obtained an inheritance, having been predestined according to His purpose who works all things after the counsel of His will…

—Ephesians 1:4–5, 11, NASB

For we are His workmanship, created in Christ Jesus for good works, which God prepared beforehand so that we would walk in them… So then you are no longer strangers and aliens, but you are fellow citizens with the saints, and are of God's household…

—Ephesians 2:10, 19, NASB

Your value comes from God, not other people's opinions—or even your own opinions.

A Chart of Losses and God's Remedies

Loss	Biblical Scripture
Hope	"For I know the plans I have for you," declares the Lord, "plans to prosper you and not to harm you, plans to give you hope and a future." (Jeremiah 29:11)

Feeling Safe	When the Lord takes pleasure in anyone's way, he causes their enemies to make peace with them. (Proverbs 16:7)
Purpose/Ambition	I will instruct you and teach you in the way you should go; I will counsel you with my loving eye on you. (Psalm 32:8)
Effectiveness	In their hearts humans plan their course, but the Lord establishes their steps. (Proverbs 16:9)
Courage	It's better to be wise than strong; intelligence outranks muscle any day. Strategic planning is the key to warfare; to win, you need a lot of good counsel. (Proverbs 24:5, MSG)
Strength	In repentance and rest is your salvation, in quietness and trust is your strength… (Isaiah 30:15)
Self-Esteem	For you created my inmost being; you knit me together in my mother's womb. I praise you because I am fearfully and wonderfully made; your works are wonderful, I know that full well. (Psalm 139:13–14)
Control	You will keep in perfect peace those whose minds are steadfast, because they trust in you. (Isaiah 26:3)
Plans and Dreams	Trust in the Lord with all your heart and lean not on your own understanding; in all your ways submit to him, and he will make your paths straight. (Proverbs 3:5–6)
Identity	For he chose us in him before the creation of the world to be holy and blameless in his sight. (Ephesians 1:4)

Focusing on our relationship with God takes our focus away from the trauma. Changing the direction of the mind is critical to healing the mind. It renews our relationship with God.

As you grieve, it is important that you also discover your new identity as a child of God. You *are* a child of God, and God cares a great deal about you.

FINDING WORDS TO DESCRIBE YOUR TRAUMA CAN LEAD TO TRANSFORMATION

(Please circle relevant words for your emotions)

Abandoned	Crazy	Empty	Jealous
Accused	Criticized	Evil	Left Out
Agony	Deceived	Foolish	Little
Alienated	Degraded	Forced	Lonely
Alone	Demeaned	Frustrated	Lustful
Angry	Demoralized	Ganged up on	Manipulated
Apprehensive	Denial	Grief	Minimized
Anxious	Dependent	Hated	Nasty
At Fault	Depressed	Heartbroken	Needy
Ashamed	Deprived	Helpless	No Choice
Attacked	Despair	Horror	Not Approved Of
Battered	Desolate	Hurt	Not Cared For
Beaten	Destroyed	Hyperalert	Not Comforted
Belittled	Devastated	Inadequate	Not Safe
Betrayed	Different	Incompetent	Numb
Bitter	Dirty	Imprisoned	Offended
Can't Concentrate	Disappointed	Innocent	Out of Control
Cheated	Disgraced	Insecure	Overwhelmed
Condemned	Disillusioned	Irrelevant	Panicky
Confused	Disrespected	Irresponsible	Passionless
Controlled	Embarrassed	Irritable	Powerless
Pressured	Scorned	Suffocated	Unlovable
Put Down	Seduced	Terrified	Unsure
Raped	Selfish	Thrown Away	Unwanted
Rejected	Shamed	Timid	Used

Repulsed	Shattered	Tiny	Violated
Resented	Silenced	Tormented	Vulnerable
Ripped Apart	Silent Witnesses	Tossed Aside	Weak
Ruined	Small	Trapped	
Scared	Stupid	Unprotected	

Cognitive therapy is based on the cognitive model, which states that thoughts, feelings and behavior are all connected, and that individuals can move toward overcoming difficulties and meeting their goals by identifying and changing unhelpful or inaccurate thinking, problematic behavior, and distressing emotional responses.[17]

Research shows that cognitive therapy affects the deeper circuits of the brain. Putting feelings into words moves the brain into a deeper area of thinking.

PRAYER

Heavenly Father, the Bible says that You made me and that You are familiar with all my ways. You know my inner turmoil as well as the thoughts and experiences that torment me. I pray that You would help me to heal from the damage that has been done to me. Please provide me with the wisdom and resources I need to get well. Give me the courage and strength to keep going. In Jesus' name, amen.

---

17 *Wikipedia*, "Cognitive therapy." Date of access: June 1, 2017 (https://en.wikipedia.org/wiki/Cognitive_therapy).

CHAPTER FOUR

The Inner Person: Your Spiritual Self

Spiritual Symptoms of PTSD

The following is a list of spiritual symptoms of PTSD. Please check all that apply to you:

- ☐ blaming God.
- ☐ losing your trust in God.
- ☐ losing your belief in God.

Spiritual Help from God

For though we live in the world, we do not wage war as the world does. The weapons we fight with are not the weapons of the world. On the contrary, they have divine power to demolish strongholds. We demolish arguments and every pretension that sets itself up against the knowledge of God, and we take captive every thought to make it obedient to Christ.

—2 Corinthians 10:3–5

A stronghold can be likened to a "schema," which is why our thought processes occur as they do. Schemas usually pertain to the experiences we have had in our lives. In other words, there is a reason why you think the way you do.

Schema: a mental codification of experience that includes a particular organized way of perceiving cognitively and responding to a complex situation or set of stimuli.[18]

Observe your thoughts rather than react to them.

---

18 *Merriam-Webster*, "Schema." Date of access: June 1, 2017 (https://www.merriam-webster.com/dictionary/renounce).

Spiritual Battle Gear: The Armor of God (Ephesians 6:10–11)

- The belt of truth is buckled around your waist.
- The breastplate of righteousness is in place.
- Your feet are shod with the readiness that comes from the gospel of peace.
- The shield of faith extinguishes all the flaming arrows of the evil one.
- The helmet of salvation is upon your head.
- The sword of the spirit, the Word of God, is upon your lips.

PRAYER

Heavenly Father, I put on the whole armor of God. I put on the helmet of salvation and take every thought captive to the obedience of Christ. I put on the belt of truth and the breastplate of righteousness. I pick up the shield of faith. I do these things by reading Your Word, praying that You will enable me to overcome the struggles I currently face. I accept Your help through faith and choose to live by Your principles. Thank You that You have provided a way for me to get well. In Jesus' name, amen.

Spiritual Blessings in Christ (Ephesians 1:3–23)

- God has blessed us in the heavenly realms with every spiritual blessing in Christ.
- He gives us the spirit of wisdom and revelation so that we may know Him better.
- God gives us understanding so that we will know the hope of His calling.
- He gave His incomparably great power to those who believe. That power is the same as the mighty strength He exerted when He raised Christ from the dead and seated Him at His right hand in the heavenly realms.
- God put *all* things under Jesus' feet and appointed Him to be the head over the church.

For our struggle is not against flesh and blood, but against the rulers, against the authorities, against the powers of this dark world and against the spiritual forces of evil in the heavenly realms. Therefore put on the full armor of God, so that when the day of evil comes, you may be able to stand your ground, and after you have done everything, to stand.

—Ephesians 6:12–13

CHAPTER FIVE

The Areas of the Brain and What You Should Know About Them

Researchers agree that there are three regions of the brain. Integrating the brain involves linking the activity of these regions.

What follows is a brief description of each region. The purpose of my workbook is to provide a workable plan to alleviate some of the challenges for the traumatized person. With this purpose in mind, I am choosing to focus on the prefrontal cortex and the amygdala. For a further in-depth study regarding the mind and the brain, please refer to Dr. Daniel Siegel's books *Mindsight*, *The Mindful Brain*, and *The Developing Mind*.

The brain stem:

- houses the sympathetic system.
- houses the parasympathetic system.
- balances the activation and regulation of the physical structures.

The limbic system:

- evaluates our current situation.
- is the emotional control center of the brain (the driver).
- regulates the emotional structures.
- contains the amygdala, hippocampus, and hypothalamus.
- encodes emotionally charged experiences.
- forms the key mental models (schemas) about one's self, others, and the world.
- holds conditioned emotional responses (your responses based on previous experience).

The cortex:

- creates more intricate firing patterns.

- the frontal portion of the cortex allows us to have ideas, concepts, and insight into the inner world.
- the frontal cortex makes firing patterns that allow us to think about thinking.
- the prefrontal cortex creates representations of concepts such as time, a sense of self, and moral judgments.
- the prefrontal cortex participates in generating the conscious focus of attention.
- the prefrontal cortex helps coordinate and balance the firing patterns from the many regions in the brain.
- the middle prefrontal region connects everything.
- the middle prefrontal region creates links among the cortex, limbic areas, the brainstem, and the internally distributed nervous system.

Dr. Daniel J. Siegel, author of *Mindsight: The New Science of Personal Transformation*, coined the phrase "snagging the brain." Activating neurons from different brain regions creates different linkages between the brain regions. Snag stands for stimulating, neuronal, activiation, and growth.[19]

There is a popular expression that says, "Neurons that fire together, wire together."

This clever phrase was first used in 1949 by Donald Hebb, a Canadian neuropsychologist known for his work in the field of associative learning.

Hebb's axiom reminds us that every experience, thought, feeling, and physical sensation triggers thousands of neurons, which form a neural network...[20]

Experiences change the way we perceive, perform, think and plan. They do so physically by changing the structure of the nervous system, alternating neural circuits that participate in perceiving, performing, thinking and planning... Certainly our environment influences how we react to it, and our reactions influence our environment...

At the neural level, many different types of changes can be imagined...

The idea that connections between neurons that are simultaneously active are strengthened is often referred to as "Hebbian Learning"...[21]

By working in the worksheets provided herein, you will be able to connect what you're thinking to how you're feeling. Then you can figure out what to do about it. By developing linkages to the different parts of the brain, you can create activation and extend some of the prefrontal cortex circuits.

---

19 Siegel, Daniel J., M.D., *Mindsight: The New Science of Personal Transformation* (Toronto, ON: Bantam, 2009).

20 *SuperCamp*, "What Does 'Neurons that Fire Together Wire Together' Mean?" Date of access: June 1, 2017 (http://www.supercamp.com/what-does-neurons-that-fire-together-wire-together-mean/).

21 *Cornell.edu*, "Hebbian Learning and Plasticity." Date of access: June 1, 2017 (https://courses.cit.cornell.edu/bionb330/Class_notes_PARTIII.pdf).

The job of the prefrontal cortex is to focus attention on the external world and what is happening in the brain stem (the sensations and feelings coming up from your body). It also focuses your attention to your perception and memories. By observing, describing, evaluating, and reflecting on your experiences, you can learn to disengage from the automatic behaviors that cause you distress.

THE PREFRONTAL CORTEX EFFECTS OF PTSD

The following is a list of some of the effects of PTSD to the prefrontal cortex of the brain. Please check all that apply to you:

- [ ] short attention span (which often causes a person's mind to go blank in conversation)
- [ ] short-term memory problems
- [ ] impulsiveness
- [ ] disorganization
- [ ] apathy
- [ ] hyperactivity
- [ ] chronic lateness
- [ ] poor judgment
- [ ] poor time management
- [ ] procrastination
- [ ] misperceptions
- [ ] lack of empathy
- [ ] lack of insight
- [ ] trouble activating the prefrontal cortex under stress
- [ ] trouble focusing

Dear friend, guard Clear Thinking and Common Sense with your life; don't for a minute lose sight of them. They'll keep your soul alive and well, they'll keep you fit and attractive. You'll travel safely, you'll neither tire nor trip. You'll take afternoon naps without a worry, you'll enjoy a good night's sleep. No need to panic over alarms or surprises, or predictions that doomsday's just around the corner, because God will be right there with you; he'll keep you safe and sound. (Proverbs 3:21–26, MSG)

Questions About Developing the Prefrontal Cortex[22]

By answering the following questions—and keeping them in a place where you can regularly see them—you will be able to step back from current thoughts and patterns and say, "Wait a minute, what's going on here? I need to do something different to change this."

1. What would you like to accomplish in regards to health/relationships/work?

   _____

   _____

   _____

22 See www.amenclinics.com

2. What is significant and important to you?

_____

_____

_____

3. What exactly do you want? (Be specific.)

_____

_____

_____

4. What would you like to spend your time and energy on?

_____

_____

_____

5. What would bring meaning and purpose to your life?

_____

_____

_____

6. What would bring excitement and stimulation to your life to prevent shutdown?

_____

_____

_____

7. What are some limitations and boundaries that you could implement in your life to prevent burnout?

_____

_____

_____

8. What overwhelming tasks can you break down into small tasks?

_____

_____

_____

9. What turmoil are you *feeding* that you should be *starving*?

_____

_____

_____

10. What do you need to do to get where you want to go?

_____

_____

_____

11. What is the precise challenge?

_____

_____

_____

CHAPTER SIX

The Effects of PTSD on the Amygdala

The Emotions that Cause Turmoil in the Amygdala

The amygdala is a part of the brain that labels incoming stimuli from the external world, and also what's happening in the body. It labels things as "safe" or "dangerous." The amygdala links emotions, behaviors, and physical sensations together.

The following is a list of some of the emotions that cause turmoil in the amygdala. Please check all that apply to you:

- ☐ fear
- ☐ anxiety
- ☐ worry
- ☐ resentment
- ☐ bitterness
- ☐ unforgiveness

The following are physical tasks you can perform to calm the amygdala:

- Identify and analyze your emotions.
- Be completely honest about your feelings.
- Give your feelings a name.
- Work through your emotions with God through prayer.
- Give what is crushing you to Jesus.
- Change your self-talk (stop putting yourself down).
- Have empathy for yourself.
- Give yourself time to get well.

Are you tired? Worn out? Burned out on religion? Come to me. Get away with me and you'll recover your life. I'll show you how to take a real rest. Walk with me and work with me—watch how I do it. Learn the unforced rhythms of grace. I won't lay anything heavy or ill-fitting on you. Keep company with me and you'll learn to live freely and lightly

—Matthew 11:28–30 MSG

Understanding Fear

Fear: a distressing emotion aroused by impending danger, evil, pain, etc., whether the threat is real or imagined; the feeling or condition of being afraid.[23]

The Things I Fear, and the People I Fear	When, Where, and Why Am I Afraid?	Scriptures Pertaining to Fear
For example: failure, rejection, disapproval, going crazy, confrontation, pain, death, not being loved, financial loss, judgment, criticism, etc.		*Find a specific verse in the Bible that addresses your fear.*

---

23 *Dictionary.com*, "Fear." Date of access: June 1, 2017 (http://www.dictionary.com/browse/fear).

Questions About Analyzing Your Fears

1. Out of all the things you fear, which ones do you think are reasonable and which ones seem unreasonable?

_____

_____

_____

2. Have you been living under the control of fear rather than by faith in God?

_____

_____

_____

3. If you are afraid of certain people, what hold do they have over you?

_____

_____

_____

4. Are you more afraid of people than trusting in God and His help?

_____

_____

_____

Be merciful to me, my God, for my enemies are in hot pursuit; all day long they press their attack. My adversaries pursue me all day long; in their pride many are attacking me. When I am afraid, I put my trust in you. In God, whose word I praise—in God I trust and am not afraid. What can mere mortals do to me? All day long they twist my words; all their schemes are for my ruin. They conspire, they lurk, they watch my steps, hoping to take my life. Because of their wickedness do not let them escape; in your anger, God, bring the nations down. Record my misery; list my tears on your scroll—are they not in your record? Then my enemies will turn back when I call for help. By this I will know that God is for me.

—Psalms 56:1–9

PRAYER

Heavenly Father, the things I fear and the people I fear are: _____.
I repent and renounce these fears and ask You to break the power they hold over me. In Jesus' Name, Amen.

When you pass through the waters, I will be with you; and when you pass through the rivers, they will not sweep over you. When you walk through the fire, you will not be burned; the flames will not set you ablaze. For I am the Lord your God, the Holy One of Israel, your Savior; I give Egypt for your ransom, Cush and Seba in your stead.

—Isaiah 43:2–3

I sought the Lord, and he answered me; he delivered me from all my fears.

—Psalms 34:4

IDENTIFYING ANXIETY TRIGGERS

Anxiety: apprehensive uneasiness or nervousness usually over an impending or anticipated ill… medical: an abnormal and overwhelming sense of apprehension and fear often marked by physical signs (such as tension, sweating, and increased pulse rate), by doubt concerning the reality and nature of threat, and by self-doubt about one's capacity to cope with it.[24]

---

24 *Merriam-Webster*, "Anxiety." Date of access: June 1, 2017 (https://www.merriam-webster.com/dictionary/anxiety).

Physiological Reaction	What Was Occurring at the Time of the Anxiety?	Facts Relating to the Situation	Assumptions Relating to the Situation	How Can You Decrease the Threat of Danger?
For example: rapid heartbeat, dry mouth, increased blood pressure, jumpiness, feeling faint, excessive perspiring, feeling clammy, etc.	For example: conflicting life messages, unresolved conflict, adjusting poorly to changes, tense feelings, etc.			

Questions About Analyzing Your Anxieties

1. Is there a particular time of day, night, or season when you experience anxiety?

_____

_____

_____

2. What types of situations make you anxious?

_____

_____

_____

3. Is there a specific personality type that causes you anxiety?

_____

_____

_____

4. Do you know why you suffer from anxiety? In other words, do you know the root cause of your anxiety?

_____

_____

_____

5. How have you previously tried to cope with anxiety?

_____

_____

_____

6. What would your life be like if you were free from anxiety?

_____

_____

_____

7. When do your feelings of anxiety go away?

_____

_____

_____

PRAYER

Heavenly Father, I am anxious about _____. I repent and renounce these things that make me anxious and pray that You would give me victory in this area of my life. In Jesus' name, amen.

Do not be anxious about anything, but in every situation, by prayer and petition, with thanksgiving, present your requests to God. And the peace of God, which transcends all understanding, will guard your hearts and your minds in Christ Jesus.

—Philippians 4:6–7

Anxiety weighs down the heart, but a kind word cheers it up.

—Proverbs 12:25

If you don't know what you're doing, pray to the Father. He loves to help. You'll get his help, and won't be condescended to when you ask for it. Ask boldly, believingly, without a second thought. People who "worry their prayers" are like wind-whipped waves. Don't think you're going to get anything from the Master that way, adrift at sea, keeping all your options open.

—James 1:5–8, MSG

THE WORRY WHEEL

Worry: to think about problems or unpleasant things that might happen in a way that makes you feel unhappy and frightened…[25]

Who I Worry About, What I Worry About	When Do You Worry?	Scriptures Pertaining to Worry
		(See examples on the following pages.)

---

25 *Cambridge Dictionary*, "Worry." Date of access: June 1, 2017 (http://dictionary.cambridge.org/dictionary/english/worry)

> **Note:**
>
> Worry is *not* an emotion. It is a mental exercise.
>
> Worry is what you feel when you assume responsibilities that are not yours. Worry erases the promises of God from your mind.
>
> "Worry is like a rocking chair; it will give you something to do, but it won't get you anywhere." (Unknown)

PRAYER

Heavenly Father, I am worried about *(list your answers from the previous chart)*. Worrying does not solve anything; it just keeps me twirling everything around in my mind. My worries are not too big for You, and I am important to You. Worry robs me of joy and the full life You desire for me to have. I repent and renounce all of these worries, Lord, and ask You to help me overcome this bad habit. I also ask that You would enable me to consciously choose to stop worrying and to talk with You instead. I do have control over whether I worry or not. Your Word says that You will take care of me, and worrying has never helped or changed any of the outcomes anyway. In Jesus' name, amen.

SCRIPTURES ABOUT WORRY

Then Jesus said to his disciples: "Therefore I tell you, do not worry about your life, what you will eat; or about your body, what you will wear. For life is more than food, and the body more than clothes."
—Luke 12:22–23

Give your entire attention to what God is doing right now, and don't get worked up about what may or may not happen tomorrow. God will help you deal with whatever hard things come up when the time comes.
—Matthew 6:34, MSG

For the Spirit God gave us does not make us timid, but gives us power, love and self-discipline
—2 Timothy 1:7

UNDERSTANDING PANIC ATTACKS

The chart below will help you to:

1. make the connection between your physical symptoms and your thoughts.
2. replace your negative thoughts with more appropriate thoughts.
3. shut down panic attacks with deep breathing and accurate self-talk.

Physical Symptoms	Emotions	Where Were You? Who Were You With? What Was Happening?	Change Your Self-Talk and Take a Different Action
Heart palpitations	List specific fears (see examples listed below)		
Chest pains	Dying		Panic attacks cannot cause death (i.e. a heart attack).
Trembling/shaking	Going crazy		No one can go crazy from having a panic attack.
Dizziness	Fainting/passing out		If you faint, your respiratory system will kick in.

Shortness of breath/a choking feeling	Suffocating		Breathe deeply (at least ten times) and your body will reset itself.
Cold chills/hot flashes			
Unreality			
Numbing			
Tingling sensations			

ANGER, RESENTMENT, BITTERNESS, AND UNFORGIVENESS

The chart below will help you identify the source of your anger, resentment, bitterness, and unforgiveness.

I am angry at:	Because of:	I feel:
a person, situation, or event; an imaginary or anticipated event; or memories of traumatic and enraging situations.	a real or perceived injustice or hurt in the form of frustration, betrayal, deprivation, injustice, exploitation, manipulation, criticism, violence, disapproval, humiliation, or threats.	refer to pages 20-21 if you struggle to find words for your emotions.

PRAYER

Heavenly Father, I am angry at *(list answers from previous chart)* for *(list the specific events from previous chart)*. I feel *(list all of your specific emotions)*. I renounce these events that have caused me pain and I repent of my anger, bitterness, and resentment. I choose to forgive _____ for _____ and all the pain that they have inflicted upon me. Please heal my emotions of _____. I am forgiving in order that I may get well. If I am holding bitterness towards You and/or myself, please help me to identify the specific reasons for this. Help me to resolve all of my unforgiveness. In Jesus' name, amen.

Facts About Forgiveness

- The process of healing deep wounds requires plenty of time to grieve.
- Forgiveness is an intentional, focused decision we make in order to make it a reality in our lives.
- It is both an event and a process.
- God takes us through the grieving process at our own pace and in His own way.
- Excusing and minimizing is not the same as forgiving (it is called avoidance).
- We extend forgiveness regardless whether the other person acknowledges their fault.
- Forgiveness does not require that we set ourselves up for more hurt.
- Forgiveness, trust, and reconciliation are separate matters.

ANGER TRIGGERS

Who and What Makes Me Angry?	How Do I Currently Express My Anger?	What Can I Do to Delay and Calm My Anger?	How Can I Express My Anger in Constructive Ways?
		Take a temporary timeout.	
		Perform light exercise until the intensity of anger is manageable.	

		Write.	
		Talk with a trusted friend.	
		Ask God to give you insight.	

Note:

Until you can control your anger, you should avoid triggers as much as possible.

People who repress their anger are often depressed, anxious, hostile, or have other psychological and biological problems.

Those who express their anger in unhelpful ways will devastate their relationships with others.

Anger leads to resentment (resentment is anger with a history), which then turns to bitterness or hostility.

Questions About Anger Management

1. Do you have any health issues related to anger?

_____

_____

_____

2. Could you have buried anger from your past that hasn't been resolved?

_____

_____

_____

3. Are you currently acting out your anger? If so, are you acting it out as it was modeled in your growing up years?

_____

_____

_____

4. How do you think the people experiencing your anger are feeling?

_____

_____

_____

5. Do others see anger in you that you're not aware of?

_____

_____

_____

6. Have you spoken with anyone about your anger?

_____

_____

7. Have you asked God to help you with your anger?

_____

_____

_____

"In your anger do not sin": Do not let the sun go down while you are still angry, and do not give the devil a foothold.

—Ephesians 4:26–27

My dear brothers and sisters, take note of this: Everyone should be quick to listen, slow to speak and slow to become angry, because human anger does not produce the righteousness that God desires.

—James 1:19–20

Do not make friends with a hot-tempered person, do not associate with one easily angered, or you may learn their ways and get yourself ensnared.

—Proverbs 22:24–25

CHAPTER SEVEN

BIBLICAL RESTRUCTURING: ALLOWING GOD TO CHANGE YOUR MIND

GOD'S ROLE IN OUR THINKING PATTERNS

- Research shows that a child who is loved has a different brain from that of child who has been unloved.
- In changing our thought processes, it is very important to understand God's mercy, grace, love, and kindness.
- My personal recommendation is to look up scripture references about God's love and to study the books of Galatians and Ephesians in order to become better acquainted with your Savior.

And do not be conformed to this world, but be transformed by the renewing of your mind, so that you may prove what the will of God is, that which is good and acceptable and perfect.

—Romans 12:2, NASB

I ask you, therefore, not to be discouraged because of my sufferings for you, which are your glory.

For this reason I kneel before the Father, from whom every family in heaven and on earth derives its name. I pray that out of his glorious riches he may strengthen you with power through his Spirit in your inner being, so that Christ may dwell in your hearts through faith. And I pray that you, being rooted and established in love, may have power, together with all the Lord's holy people, to grasp how wide and long and high and deep is the love of Christ, and to know this love that surpasses knowledge—that you may be filled to the measure of all the fullness of God.

—Ephesians 3:13–19

CONNECTION LEADS TO VICTORY: KEEP IT SIMPLE

- By connecting to God's power, He supplies the ability to live life with a power, truth, and strength we do not possess on our own.
- When you anchor yourself to God, you're in a safe and secure place.
- Figure out what's complicating your life and learn how can you resolve it.
- Always talk with God about your ideas, thoughts, feelings, and concerns.
- Give Jesus your burdens every day.
- Include Him in every element of your life.
- Ask God to take away the things that drain you.
- Approach Him as you really are, not who you think you should be.
- Look for God's comfort and security. He knows how to provide for your needs.
- Set aside time to be silent and still with the Lord.

God, my shepherd! I don't need a thing. You have bedded me down in lush meadows, you find me quiet pools to drink from. True to your word, you let me catch my breath and send me in the right direction. Even when the way goes through Death Valley, I'm not afraid when you walk at my side. Your trusty shepherd's crook makes me feel secure. You serve me a six-course dinner right in front of my enemies. You revive my drooping head; my cup brims with blessing. Your beauty and love chase after me every day of my life. I'm back home in the house of God for the rest of my life.

—Psalm 23, MSG

For the eyes of the Lord range throughout the earth to strengthen those whose hearts are fully committed to him.

—2 Chronicles 16:9

I am the true vine, and My Father is the vinedresser. Every branch in Me that does not bear fruit, He takes away; and every branch that bears fruit, He prunes it so that it may bear more fruit. You are already clean because of the word which I have spoken to you. Abide in Me, and I in you. As the branch cannot bear fruit of itself unless it abides in the vine, so neither can you unless you abide in Me.

—John 15:1–4, NASB

But seek first His kingdom and His righteousness, and all these things will be added to you.

—Matthew 6:33, NASB

Trust God from the bottom of your heart; don't try to figure out everything on your own. Listen for God's voice in everything you do, everywhere you go; he's the one who will keep you on track. Don't assume that you know it all. Run to God! Run from evil! Your body will glow with health, your very bones will vibrate with life! Honor God with everything you own; give him the first and the best. Your barns will burst, your wine vats will brim over. But don't, dear friend, resent God's discipline; don't sulk under his loving correction. It's the child he loves that God corrects; a father's delight is behind all this.

—Proverbs 3:5–12, MSG

In my own life, I have found that the Lord often has a strategy that I don't understand. I have also come to accept that I don't have to figure it all out. I often drove myself over the edge trying to figure out what to do. In hindsight, I have learned to pray about all issues concerning me. By asking for His wisdom and trusting in His guidance, I have been able to move from chaos to peace.

I have told you these things, so that in me you may have peace. In this world you will have trouble. But take heart! I have overcome the world.

—John 16:33

A BIBLICAL EXAMPLE OF GOD'S PROVISION

One example of God's provision can be found by reading the story of Elijah. Elijah was both physically exhausted and emotionally spent. When he was running for his life, God sent him to a safe place where He protected and provided for him. God hid Elijah for three years.

Consider the ravens, for they neither sow nor reap; they have no storeroom nor barn, and yet God feeds them; how much more valuable you are than the birds!

—Luke 12:24, NASB

A BIBLICAL EXAMPLE OF TRAUMA: THE APOSTLE PAUL

Five times I received from the Jews thirty-nine lashes. Three times I was beaten with rods, once I was stoned, three times I was shipwrecked, a night and a day I have spent in the deep. I have been on frequent journeys, in dangers from rivers, dangers from robbers, dangers from my countrymen, dangers from the Gentiles, dangers in the city, dangers in the wilderness, dangers on the sea, dangers among false brethren; I have been in labor and hardship, through many sleepless nights, in hunger and thirst, often without food, in cold and exposure.

—2 Corinthians 11:24–27, NASB

And He has said to me, "My grace is sufficient for you, for power is perfected in weakness." Most gladly, therefore, I will rather boast about my weaknesses, so that the power of Christ may dwell in me. Therefore I am well content with weaknesses, with insults, with distresses, with persecutions, with difficulties, for Christ's sake; for when I am weak, then I am strong.

—2 Corinthians 12:9–10, NASB

But we have this treasure in earthen vessels, so that the surpassing greatness of the power will be of God and not from ourselves; we are afflicted in every way, but not crushed; perplexed, but not despairing; persecuted, but not forsaken; struck down, but not destroyed; always carrying about in the body the dying of Jesus, so that the life of Jesus also may be manifested in our body.

—2 Corinthians 4:7–10, NASB

PRAYER

Lord, I can't get over, or past, *(list your feelings or experiences)* I am weak in this regard. Please give me Your strength and Your grace.

MEDITATE ON SCRIPTURE

The Lord is my rock, my fortress and my deliverer; my God is my rock, in whom I take refuge, my shield and the horn of my salvation, my stronghold. I called to the Lord, who is worthy of praise, and I have been saved from my enemies. The cords of death entangled me; the torrents of destruction overwhelmed me. The cords of the grave coiled around me; the snares of death confronted me. In my distress I called to the Lord; I cried to my God for help. From his temple he heard my voice; my cry came before him, into his ears.

—Psalms 18:2–6

I will go before you and make the rough places smooth; I will shatter the doors of bronze and cut through their iron bars. I will give you the treasures of darkness and hidden wealth of secret places, so that you may know that it is I, the Lord, the God of Israel, who calls you by your name.

—Isaiah 45:2–3, NASB

Praise the Lord, my soul; all my inmost being, praise his holy name. Praise the Lord, my soul, and forget not all his benefits—who forgives all your sins and heals all your diseases, who redeems your life from the pit and crowns you with love and compassion, who satisfies your desires with good things so that your youth is renewed like the eagle's. The Lord works righteousness and justice for all the oppressed.

—Psalm 103:1–6

The cords of death entangled me, the anguish of the grave came over me; I was overcome by distress and sorrow. Then I called on the name of the Lord: "Lord, save me!" The Lord is gracious and righteous; our God is full of compassion. The Lord protects the unwary; when I was brought low, he saved me. Return to your rest, my soul, for the Lord has been good to you.

—Psalm 116:3–7

Scorn has broken my heart and has left me helpless; I looked for sympathy, but there was none, for comforters, but I found none.

—Psalm 69:20

Look and see, there is no one at my right hand; no one is concerned for me. I have no refuge; no one cares for my life. I cry to you, Lord; I say, "You are my refuge, my portion in the land of the living.

—Psalm 142:4–5

Lord, you are the God who saves me; day and night I cry out to you. May my prayer come before you; turn your ear to my cry.

I am overwhelmed with troubles and my life draws near to death. I am counted among those who go down to the pit; I am like one without strength. I am set apart with the dead, like the slain who lie in the grave, whom you remember no more, who are cut off from your care.

You have put me in the lowest pit, in the darkest depths. Your wrath lies heavily on me; you have overwhelmed me with all your waves. You have taken from me my closest friends and have made me repulsive to them. I am confined and cannot escape; my eyes are dim with grief.

I call to you, Lord, every day; I spread out my hands to you. Do you show your wonders to the dead? Do their spirits rise up and praise you? Is your love declared in the grave, your faithfulness in Destruction? Are your wonders known in the place of darkness, or your righteous deeds in the land of oblivion?

But I cry to you for help, Lord; in the morning my prayer comes before you. Why, Lord, do you reject me and hide your face from me?

From my youth I have suffered and been close to death; I have borne your terrors and am in despair. Your wrath has swept over me; your terrors have destroyed me. All day long they surround me like a flood; they have completely engulfed me. You have taken from me friend and neighbor—darkness is my closest friend.

—Psalm 88:1–18

You may say to yourselves, "These nations are stronger than we are. How can we drive them out?" But do not be afraid of them; remember well what the Lord your God did to Pharaoh and to all Egypt. You saw with your own eyes the great trials, the signs and wonders, the mighty hand and outstretched arm, with which the Lord your God brought you out. The Lord your God will do the same to all the peoples you now fear. Moreover, the Lord your God will send the hornet among them until even the survivors who hide from you have perished. Do not be terrified by them, for the Lord your God, who is among you, is a great and awesome God. The Lord your God will drive out those nations before you, little by little. You will not be allowed to eliminate them all at once, or the wild animals will multiply around you. But the Lord your God will deliver them over to you, throwing them into great confusion until they are destroyed.

—Deuteronomy 7:17–23

Whoever dwells in the shelter of the Most High will rest in the shadow of the Almighty. I will say of the Lord, "He is my refuge and my fortress, my God, in whom I trust."

Surely he will save you from the fowler's snare and from the deadly pestilence. He will cover you with his feathers, and under his wings you will find refuge; his faithfulness will be your shield and rampart. You will not fear the terror of night, nor the arrow that flies by day, nor the pestilence that stalks in the darkness, nor the plague that destroys at midday. A thousand may fall at your side, ten thousand at your right hand, but it will not come near you. You will only observe with your eyes and see the punishment of the wicked.

If you say, "The Lord is my refuge," and you make the Most High your dwelling, no harm will overtake you, no disaster will come near your tent. For he will command his angels concerning you to guard you in all your ways; they will lift you up in their hands, so that you will not strike your foot against a stone. You will tread on the lion and the cobra; you will trample the great lion and the serpent.

"Because he loves me," says the Lord, "I will rescue him; I will protect him, for he acknowledges my name. He will call on me, and I will answer him; I will be with him in trouble, I will deliver him and honor him. With long life I will satisfy him and show him my salvation."

—Psalm 91:1–16

PRAYER

Heavenly Father, I have learned a lot and sometimes I am overwhelmed. Enable me to process everything and to understand that healing can take a long time. Help me to be patient with myself. Give me the ability to see myself as You see me. Jesus said that we should come to Him when we are weary and burdened. I come to You now, Jesus, and ask You to give me rest for my soul. Help me to do what You require as You are gentle and humble in heart. Give me a desire to grow close to You, and I ask You to walk the road of life with me. I ask for wisdom in all aspects of myself and my life. In Jesus' name, amen.

CHAPTER EIGHT

OVERVIEW OF HEALING FROM TRAUMA: A BIBLICAL PERSPECTIVE

Practical Tips for Healing from Trauma

1. Build or rebuild your relationship with your Creator.
2. Maintain your overall physical and emotional health.
3. Simplify your life.
4. Slow down and enjoy your life.
5. Do things that make life fun and interesting.
6. Hope, dream, and envision new possibilities.
7. Get creative.
8. When you have made peace with your past, try not to get pulled back into it.

GOD'S VALUES BRING PEACE AND WELL-BEING

The Old Self (Without Christ) Ephesians 4:17–24 Colossians 3:1–15	The New Self (With Christ) Ephesians 4:17–24 Colossians 3:1–15
You had darkened understanding and futility of thinking.	You are made new in the attitude of your minds. Walk in a manner worthy of the calling with which you have been called.
You were excluded from the life of God because of the hardness of your heart.	You are reconciled to God because of His mercy. You have the peace of Christ.

You were corrupted in accordance with the lusts of deceit.	You have a heart of compassion, kindness, and love.
You had lost all sensitivity and were callous.	You exhibit gentleness and patience, showing humility towards all men.
You indulged in immorality, impurity, passion, evil desire, and greed, which amounts to idolatry.	You are taught by Jesus because of His love toward mankind. Let the word of Christ richly dwell within you.
You were living in malice and envy.	You forgive others as Christ has forgiven you, showing tolerance for others in love.
You were full of anger, rage, slander, and abusive speech.	You bear with others and forgive them when you have grievances.
You were carnal.	You set your minds on things above, not earthly things.

PRAYER

Heavenly Father, I repent and renounce *(list specific ways from the reference points in the above chart)* in which I have sinned. I ask for Your forgiveness and cleansing. I choose to put on the "new self" and ask You to help me obtain the fruit of Your Holy Spirit. In Jesus' name, amen.

But the fruit of the Spirit is love, joy, peace, patience, kindness, goodness, faithfulness, gentleness, self-control; against such things there is no law.

—Galatians 5:22–23, NASB

Only God can work on your soul and spirit.

Amen, Dr. Daniel G., *Change Your Brain, Change Your Life* (Toronto, ON: Harmony, 2015).

American Psychiatric Association, *Diagnostic and Statistical Manual of Mental Disorders, 5th Edition (DSM-5)* (Arlington, VA: American Psychiatric Association Publishing, 2013).

Anderson, Neil T., *Restored: Experience Life with Jesus* (Oxford, UK: Monarch Books, 2007).

Anderson, Neil T., and Rich Miller, *Freedom from Fear: Overcoming Worry and Anxiety* (Eugene, OR: Harvest House, 1999).

Clinton, Dr. Tim, Archibald Hart, and George Ohlschlager, *Caring for People God's Way: Personal and Emotional Issues, Addictions, Grief, and Trauma* (Nashville, TN: Thomas Nelson, 2005).

Clinton, Dr. Tim, and Dr. Ron Hawkins, *The Quick Reference Guide to Biblical Counseling* (Grand Rapids, MI: Baker Books, 2009).

Clinton, Dr. Tim, and Dr. Gary Sibcy, *Why You Do the Things You Do* (Nashville, TN: Thomas Nelson, 2006).

Clinton, Dr. Tim, Bob Dees, Diane Langberg, Eric Scalise, Archibald Hart, Gary Sibcy, Jennifer Cisney, and Mark Ellers, *Stress and Trauma Care with Military Application Counseling Certificate Training Program* (Forest, VA: Light University, 2016).

Cloud, Dr. Henry, *Never Go Back: 10 Things You'll Never Do Again* (Brentwood, TN: Howard, 2014)

Cloud, Dr. Henry, and Dr. John Townsend, *Boundaries: When to Say Yes, How to Say No to Take Control of Your Life* (Grand Rapids, MI: Zondervan, 2008).

Cloud, Dr. Henry, and Dr. John Townsend, *God Will Make A Way: What to Do When You Don't Know What to Do* (Nashville, TN: Thomas Nelson, 2006).

Mate, Dr. Gabor, *When the Body Says No: The Cost of Hidden Stress* (Toronto, ON: Vintage Canada, 2004).

Sibcy, Dr. Gary, *Neurobiology 2.0: Continuing Education & Professional Development Series* (Forest, VA: Light University, 2016).

Sibcy, Dr. Gary, *Panic Disorders: The Geneva Series, Professional and Continuing Education for Today's Christian Leaders* (Forest, VA: American Association of Christian Counselors, 2006).

Siegel, Daniel J., M.D., *The Developing Mind: How Relationships and the Brain Interact to Shape Who We Are* (New York, NY: The Guilford Press, 2001).

Siegel, Daniel J., M.D., *The Mindful Brain* (New York, NY: WW Norton, 2007).

Siegel, Daniel J., M.D., *Mindsight: The New Science of Personal Transformation* (Toronto, ON: Bantam, 2009).

Swindoll, Charles R., and David Lien, *Elijah: A Man of Heroism and Humility* (Plano, TX: Insight for Living, 2001).

Swindoll, Charles R., *Getting Through the Tough Stuff: It's Always Something* (Nashville, TN: Thomas Nelson, 2006).

Swindoll, Charles R., *Job: A Man of Heroic Endurance* (Nashville, TN: Thomas Nelson, 2009).

Swindoll, Charles R., and Ken Gire, *A Ministry Anyone Could Trust: A Study of 2 Corinthians 1–7* (Plano, TX: Insight for Living, 2001).

Swindoll, Charles R., and Ken Gire, *A Minister Everyone Would Respect: A Study of 2 Corinthians 8–13* (Plano, TX: Insight for Living, 2001).

Swindoll, Charles R., Mark Tobey, Marla Alupoaicei, Suzanne Keffer, and Brian Goins, *Paul: A Man of Grace and Grit* (Nashville, TN: Thomas Nelson, 2002).

van der Kolk, Bessel, *The Body Keeps The Score: Brain, Mind, and Body in the Healing of Trauma* (New York, NY: Penguin, 2015).

Wright, H. Norman, *Recovering from Losses in Life* (Grand Rapids, MI: Revell, 2006).

11/1^